Reading Pr

e	ea
get	read
then	head
them	bread
well	dread
went	meant
end	leapt
send	health
next	spread
self	ready
spend	instead

Vocabulary

dreadful – terrible

nods off – falls asleep or dozes

groans   – makes a low sound expressing pain or
                  sadness

The characters in this book are:

Liz   Matt   Tam

MATT'S BAD HEAD

Matt is sick in bed. His head hurts and he feels dreadful.

"Rest is best!" Tam tells him.

1

Matt is fed up. The rest of the band is having fun and he is stuck in bed. He nods off.

2

Matt has a bad dream. "Get away!"
he yells in his sleep. He gets up.
He is dripping with sweat.

3

"I dreamt I was attacked by a hunk of cheese. I had no weapon to defend myself!" he tells Tam.

Tam hands him bread spread with melted cheese. "I think you smelt the cheese in your sleep!"

"I can sing to help you get well,"
says Liz. "Stop, it is dreadful!"
groans Matt. "My head is better!"

Comprehension

1. Why is Matt in bed?

2. What is Matt thinking when he is stuck in bed?

3. What does Matt dream about?

4. Why do you think Matt dreamt about cheese?

5. What does Matt say when Liz starts to sing?

JUMPING JACK GAME

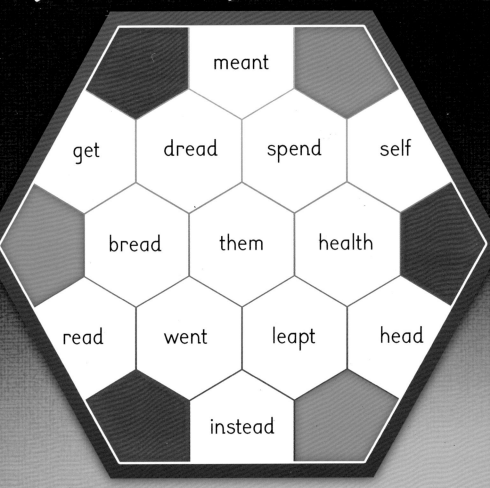

meant

get   dread   spend   self

bread   them   health

read   went   leapt   head

instead

This is a game for two players. Each player has three counters, each set a different colour. Players choose to be Red or Blue and place one counter on each of their colours.

Players take turns to move a counter by sliding it into an adjacent space or by jumping over their opponent's counter into an empty space. When a player lands on a word, he/she must read the word aloud. The winner is the first player to get all three of his/her counters in a straight line.